Permission Slips

Essential Tools for a Vibrant Life

Written by Casey Daly

Copyright © 2017 Casey Daly

All rights reserved.

No part of this book may be reproduced in any form or by any electronic or mechanical means including storage and retrieval systems, without permission in writing from the author. The only exception is by a reviewer, who may quote short excerpts in a review.

Casey Daly

visit my website at www.jarofpaper.com

First Printing May 2017

Vibrantly Focused

For the miraculous souls who fill my
echo chamber with the perfect blend of
chaos, laughter, and love.

For Sister Friend who said, "I dare you not to."

For you.
You dear, beautiful human.

Table of Contents

Introduction 2

I - Meet Your Committee 5

II - Dealing with the Committee: PQRS 14

III – Why Permission Slips Work 18

IV - You have permission 21

    1 – to allow yourself grace 22

    2 – to make noise and take up space 25

    3 – to be curious 27

    4 – to love the bully 29

    5 – to hold space for yourself 35

    6 – to be an adventurer 43

    7 – to acknowledge that you are a creator 47

    8 – to create your own echo chamber 52

    9 – to ask yourself powerful questions 55

    10 – to get out of your own way 59

    11 – to go alone 62

    12 – to create Door Number Three 65

    13 – to be your own Permission Slip Ninja 69

V – When the Struggle is REAL 71

VI – The Beginning 79

If we could change ourselves, the tendencies in the world would also change. As a man changes his own nature, so does the attitude of the world change toward him. We need not wait to see what others do.

- Mahatma Gandhi

And above all, watch with glittering eyes the whole world around you because the greatest secrets are always hidden in the most unlikely places. Those who don't believe in magic will never find it.

- Roald Dahl

Introduction

I am a child, a sibling, a spouse, a parent, and a friend.

I have at times been: unemployed, bankrupt, and depressed (not necessarily in that order).

I have cried the *ugly cry* (you know the *ugly cry*).

And - I have marveled at the blessings and the magic that surround me.

I love and am loved unconditionally.

My life and I are very human: magnificently unpredictable and imperfect.

Being human is the ultimate ride. Sometimes you're looking down on the clouds from above. Other times you will find yourself in your very own Pit of Despair. Most of the time we find ourselves just doing very human things.

There is a lot of busy work involved in being human. There is all of the eating, working, cleaning, and sleeping that have to be done every day so that you can wake up tomorrow and do it all over again. That is how most of *my* hours are spent, anyway.

Those are the hours in-between. They are in-between the times where <u>your breath is taken away</u> by either joy or despair. The hours in-between are when you have time to think.

What I found is that, as a human, time to think often led me to places that left me feeling *less than*. Less than fantastic about myself, something I had done in the past, or what I was doing now. If feeling crappy about the past or the present wasn't getting the job done, there was always something in the future that I could feel *less than* great about.

What you have here in your hands is my solution to *less than*. It has taken my hours in-between and filled them with *more*. More joy, more ease, more gratitude, more love and more compassion for myself and everyone else.

It is not hyperbole to say that the content of *Permission Slips* has completely changed the way I exist in the hours in-between. On the outside, I am still doing all of the human things (eating, working, cleaning, sleeping). The change is inside. When I am doing those things, I am lighter.

Do I still have bad days? Ummm – yes. Human. I didn't get a permission slip to get off of the roller coaster. But I am more resilient when bad days happen. It's just a bad day. It doesn't make me feel *less than* in the way that it used to. *Permission Slips: Essential Tools for a Vibrant Life* is just that - a set of tools that I use. Every. Single. Day.

Remember: It's a practice, not a panacea. The tools in this book are like a pair of running shoes in the closet. You have to use them if you want to see results.

Open your heart, open your mind, and open the book.

Open the book, open your mind, and open your heart.

With love, compassion, and humility,

Casey

I - Meet Your Committee

You were raised in a community of one kind or another.

It may have been with a perfectly functional and loving family, in a home surrounded by a white picket fence, nestled in a wonderfully diverse neighborhood where everyone got along. You may have gone to a school with no bullies, a place where everyone was always kind to you. The adults in your life (parents, teachers, coaches) didn't do anything to make you feel like you had any deficiencies. You were challenged, yet never made to feel that you were falling short of anyone's expectations.

If that is the case, on behalf of the human race, I'd like to welcome you to Earth.

The rest of us were raised in places that had widely varying levels of dysfunction.

Humans are imperfect. It is part of what makes us all so interesting. We are imperfect creatures who were raised by other imperfect creatures in imperfect communities.

Each generation (for the most part) does their best to raise the next with slightly less dysfunction than they were exposed to. Sometimes the result of that is just a different brand of dysfunction.

In any case, it's not easy being human. With a few exceptions, we're all doing the best we can.

Let's get back to this idea of community. One definition of *community* is *a group of people linked by a common policy.*

When people come together based on what is common & acceptable, they must also agree upon what is different & unacceptable (at least to a certain degree).

To be different **means** something about you. If nothing else, *different* helps to define you as being outside of the community. A community has rules, expectations, and assumptions about what is right, good (if not merely polite), and socially acceptable.

We learn these lessons as children so that we can fit into the community that raises us (dysfunctional or not). Some lessons keep us safe. Some lessons merely keep us in good standing with the community. When our community is what keeps us safe, the lessons do both.

Soon we develop a conscience (those little voices in our head) to help us keep track of right & wrong. For our purposes, think of the conscience as a small committee in our minds that assigns meaning to every action. It knows the rules of our community. It knows if an action is wrong or right, and if taking that action is going to gain us further acceptance within the community or put us in danger of being shunned.

To demonstrate *conscience as committee*, let's apply this idea to the universally human bodily function of passing gas.

Babies pass gas and it's cute. They are given praise for working out the bubble. "Awwww - doesn't that feel better, now? Nice job!"

Around the time the child reaches the age of four, the community will assume that a child has physical control over that particular bodily function. Now the very same child living in the very same community will be told that it's not okay to pass gas (fart) in front of other people. It is rude, taboo, and disgusting. A person who does that should feel shame.

It's the same person, same community, same action - new meaning. The committee in the head of the child (its conscience) now has new meaning to apply to the action *passing gas in public*: I am bad if I do that, and I should feel shame.

In many communities, girls and women are pretty strictly forbidden from passing gas in the presence of others. Ever. Some children will grow up thinking that their mom never farts.

In these same places, everyone knows that dads fart. It's okay for men. Boys will even do it on purpose when they're hanging out together to see who is the loudest and/or the most foul.

These same boys will nearly die of embarrassment if they let one slip on a date. Years later, the couple is married. That man may have no qualms about letting one rip right in front of the family (see above: *everyone knows that dads fart*).

The very same man would not fart in an office meeting; but would not hesitate when working outdoors (whether or not he knew anyone was going to hear him do it).

The point is: we learn things from the community that we are brought up in. What we learn about how to behave is dependent on things like age, gender, and situation. The committee (conscience) creates different rules for us depending on the variables.

Did the fact that I chose to demonstrate this idea by using farts bother you? If so, the Committee in your head says that talking about farts is rude, and I should be ashamed of myself for not coming up with a less vulgar way of demonstrating my point.

That's great! You're human. As humans we all have a Committee Responsible for Assigning Meaning and Provoking Shame (CRAMPS).

Your CRAMPS tells you that farts are taboo. Mine says that, too.

Your CRAMPS might even be uncomfortable with that acronym because the word *cramps* is so often associated with menstruation. The CRAMPS may declare that talking about periods is also taboo.

These are tiny assumptions that are so engrained in us that it becomes impossible to separate them from ourselves. They seem obvious.

That gets tricky though. What may seem obvious to a person from one culture may defy custom and offend in another. For example, in most Western nations a left-handed person eats food with their left hand and thinks nothing of it. The Committee assigns no meaning to it.

If that same left-handed person visits other parts of the world (India, Africa, the Middle East) and reaches for food with their left hand, the people they are dining with may be mortified. The left hand is considered unclean, and should only be used for things like cleaning one's bottom - *never* for eating food.

The Committee in those cultures applies the meaning *unclean* to eating with the left hand and provokes shame in those who do so.

The Committee is our conscience reminding us of the rules that it believes we need to play by in order to be accepted in *our* community. It would have us behave as though our very survival depends on it.

It wants you to minimize risk, blend in with the crowd - play it safe. It makes rulings on every action we take (sometimes silently, sometimes with GREAT VOLUME).

The Committee is being formed in our earliest days by both the voices and actions of the people in our community.

Much of what it rules on it does with **assumptions and beliefs** that it doesn't know the origin of, and that it sometimes doesn't even realize it has. It just thinks the way it does because that is the way it has always thought.

Many of these beliefs and assumptions don't really belong to *your* Committee. They are the opinions of someone close to you that began to feel like your own. They got picked up along the way, and you've been carrying around someone else's baggage.

Understand this: the Committee Responsible for Assigning Meaning and Provoking Shame is not a villain. It is doing the best it can (with the information it has received) to keep us safe within our community.

However, while the Committee was keeping you safe, there is a very good chance it has been *simultaneously* holding you back and stealing your joy.

This happens when the Committee is also the voice that tells you that you are: too thin or too fat, not smart enough or too brainy, not working hard enough or trying too hard. It is the voice that tells you that there are standards (impossible standards) to be met. This is the voice that will convince you that perfection is attainable – *just not by you.*

Well, enough of *that* noise.

Permission Slips is filled with tools that you can use (over and over again) to free yourself from negative self-talk and live a vibrant life. By the end, you will learn how to be grateful for your Committee - love it, even. Love it for keeping you safe for all of these years. Thank it for its hard work and steadfast dedication. Cherish its willingness to change (ever so slowly). In fact, loving your Committee is the fastest way to reform it.

You have permission to create a life based in compassion, adventure and positivity.

The journey begins here.

II - Dealing with the Committee: PQRS

This book is full of permission slips written to allow you to bypass your Committee Responsible for Assigning Meaning and Provoking Shame (CRAMPS).

It is the work of a lifetime.

Let's begin with this tool. It is a simple framework designed to help deal with the Committee and the alarms that it sets off when it is working overtime.

Here's a silly acronym to help you remember: PQRS.

> P - present
> Q - quiet
> R - release/reframe/reality
> S - start over

Here's an example of how it works:

You're looking for some feedback on something you've poured your heart & sweat into (a poem, a proposal, a prospectus). This thing is a small piece of you.

You send it to a friend (one who always responds to you in a flash). But now, a full day has passed and you've heard nothing. You assume the worst. Your heart is racing, you keep checking your email, and you are a wreck.

Your Committee is telling you that this delayed response means that what you sent was awful, and maybe you should feel a little embarrassed or ashamed about it. What can you do to talk yourself down? PQRS.

P - be present

What does that mean? Well you have to be **present** enough to your emotions to realize that you are freaking out. This can be tricky when your anxiety is running amok. It's an important first step. You can't stop yourself from freaking out if you don't know you're doing it.

Q - quiet the Committee

In this case, your mind is telling you that the delay from your friend *means* that your work is terrible. You are feeling ashamed that you even shared it. Because you are *present* enough to see that it is the

Committee setting off your internal smoke alarms (and that this is really some burnt toast and not a house fire), you can **quiet** the Committee down long enough to start thinking for yourself. No one can think when the smoke alarm is BLARING IN THEIR EAR.

R - release/reframe/reality

With the Committee quieted, you can take a more objective look at the feedback it has provided you. Then, **release** it like the garbage it is. **Reframe** your thinking using **reality** as your point of reference.

What do you really know? You sent something out. You haven't heard back. When you *release* the meaning that the Committee assigned, you can be open to the plain facts. Your friend hasn't replied to you, and that means only one thing: they haven't replied. Period. Using your mind to convince you that the delay is evidence of anything more is a disservice to you & your friend.

S - start over

Take a breath. Be in this moment with what is real and true. That is one way to **start over**. If the

Committee is still making noise, *start the process over*. The Committee may start in on the original story again, or it may assign a new meaning. It may also start telling you that this process is stupid, and that the fact that you're still freaking out *means* something about you (and about this process). That's okay. Just start over whenever/however you need to.

* If the **reality** that you hear is negative, there is a good chance that your Committee is just *tricking you* into believing that it's quiet (like kids at a slumber party).

Not sure? Try taking a few slow, deep, breaths. Was it easy? Or did you have to really make an effort? If it was like work, try relaxing before you **start over**. A state of calm is where you will do your best PQRS work. There are lots of ways to get there. Here are some suggestions:
- meditate.
- relax and deepen your breathing.
- take a short walk.
- color a picture.
- do some simple arithmetic.
- take a bath.

III – Why Permission Slips Work

You've been introduced to the Committee Responsible for Assigning Meaning and Provoking Shame (CRAMPS). And you've learned *one way* to deal with them (PQRS).

We started there; because, it's useful to have a framework to guide you. We can all use something easy to remember to help explain what is going on in our minds, and how we can manage it. Now we add permission slips.

Our minds like rules (for the most part). The Committee LOVES them. It wants us to work within the norms of our community, right? It wants to keep us safe and within the pale. So, when we begin to stray from our customary behavior, it is really useful to have permission to do so. It shuts the Committee right up.

It really doesn't matter who permission comes from (not to our Committee, anyway). When you first begin using permission slips, it seems to help when they come from someone else.

I know that I have no authority to give you permission to do anything (and so do you). That being said, I know that getting permission from an outside source has worked for me, time and again.

One time in particular: I was attending a marketing seminar. With only five minutes to prepare, we had to make up a product, create a marketing strategy and give a 4-minute sales pitch.

Panic set in. But, before he cut us loose he said, "It's not going to be perfect. You have permission to bumble and stumble through your presentation."

With those two sentences we were set free. Every one of us threw together something amazing (not perfect).

We were stunned at just how free and creative we felt once we were given permission to be imperfect. That was the real lesson.

We got "making it perfect" out of our way so that we could focus on "making it happen." That made all of the difference.

Our Committees couldn't assign any meaning to creating something imperfect, or make us feel ashamed about how much stumbling we did. All because we had permission to be imperfect.

It worked brilliantly! I would have been frozen in place if he hadn't said those words. Now when I start to get in my own way, and find myself in creative paralysis, I give myself permission to "bumble and stumble" through things. It works every time. Stuff gets done.

In fact, I have become a self-proclaimed *Permission Slip Ninja*. I use Permission Slips to covertly work around my Committee when it is holding me back.

Freedom comes from permission.

What you will find in the following pages is freedom disguised as permission slips.

If you happen upon one that you don't need, or one that rubs you the wrong way - skip it. Move on to the next one. There may be a day when you come back to it. Life is always in flux, and you never know when you're going to need permission to get out of your own way.

IV - You have permission...

1 – to allow yourself grace

One day in yoga, the instructor led us into navasana (boat pose). Not to be confused with savasana (corpse pose), which is my personal favorite.

I had been practicing yoga on and off for more than a decade, and I knew that I had this in my bag of tricks. Try as I might (and boy was I trying) I could not get my balance that day.

It is said that yoga is not a competitive sport. And it's not; except for sometimes, if you're human. If that's the case, despite your best intentions to honor the practice and Zen out, it feels a lot like a competition. At the very least, it can feel like a competition with yourself. I was striving that day: striving for the perfect boat pose.

My wonderful instructor saw me flailing with great determination. Then, with sincerity and compassion, she said to the class: "This pose may not be available to you today. That's okay."

That moment changed my life.

It may not be available to me *today* and *that's okay*. Wow. Really??

Should I give up on ever being able to hold boat pose?

No. I just don't have to strive for it today.

There was such grace in that moment for me. She was clearly not giving up on me. She knew I was capable of it. I knew I was capable of it. The reasons didn't matter. It wasn't something I could muster *that day*. And that was *okay*. *I was okay*. It didn't mean anything about my practice or me. It was simply a moment in time.

I have taken that grace into other arenas in my life. Sometimes it has to do with what I am physically capable of. Sometimes it has to do with what I am emotionally capable of. We are not always going to be on our "A game."

Allowing yourself grace when something is not available to you is not the same as making excuses. I think this is the place where grace and self-compassion sometimes get lost.

If we are responsible, accountable, and reliable we don't make excuses for ourselves. As a result, when we *are* truly challenged we may not allow ourselves grace, forgiveness, or compassion. Even if we would extend those things to anyone else who found themselves in our circumstances, we do not allow it for ourselves.

You have permission to be gentle with yourself. You have permission to allow yourself grace.

It (whatever "it" is) may not be available to you today. That's okay. You're (still) okay.

This is simply one moment in time.

This moment does not define you.

You get to define this moment (not the CRAMPS).

Do not apply meaning. Do not feel shame.

Allow grace.

2 – to make noise and take up space

Years ago, I came across a meme made to resemble an illustration from a children's book of words. It was a diagram of a young girl. Arm, leg, knee, nose, elbow, and ear: each neatly labeled. Dramatically scrawled in black marker was a line coming from the girl's face and the word: *VOICE*. It was a powerful image.

At some point, all of us will come in contact with someone who is on living on the margins, someone disenfranchised, someone invisible, someone held in silence.

Gender, race, religion, sexual orientation, disability, socioeconomic status, and age: these all play a role in how society views you. These factors determine what your Committee tells you about the space you and your voice *should* occupy.

Has it ever happened to you? Have you ever found that that you:

- undervalue your role in the lives of the people around you?

- withhold your opinion because you aren't sure it is worth sharing?
- stay small so that you don't upset anyone?

It doesn't have to be large scale.

Your CRAMPS has assigned meaning to taking up space and making noise; you feel ashamed, self conscious, or embarrassed when you do.

You have permission to use your voice. You have permission to be heard. You have permission to take up space in a room. Not just with your body, with your presence, too.

As Dr. Seuss wrote: "Be who you are and say what you feel, because those who mind don't matter and those who matter don't mind."

**If you find yourself uniquely immune to this phenomenon, please consider using your presence and your voice to help someone else value theirs.

3 – to be curious

Little kids ask a ton of questions. It can be exhausting. It is also one of my favorite things about them. They are blank slates. There is a LOT to learn about the planet, the universe it spins in, the things that live on it, the things that don't, and how to be a human.

Ask enough questions, and one day your Committee will convince you that some of them are stupid. It's nearly impossible to know which are smart and which aren't. As a result, our CRAMPS may assign the meaning "stupid" to all questions (just in case). No one wants to be seen as a dummy. In the end, we just stop asking.

I had stopped. Until one day, an episode of Sesame Street set me free. Someone said to Big Bird, "Asking questions is a good way to learn things." I decided that if Big Bird could do it, so could I.

I have learned so much by setting aside the fear and shame of not knowing everything. It makes conversation much more fulfilling. I get to learn. The people I encounter know that I am engaged and interested in what they have to say.

You have permission to not know everything. You have permission to ask questions. Because while we may have CRAMPS telling us that it's risky, we've also heard the saying: "There's no such thing as a stupid question." Believe it!

Be proud to be curious, always learning, always looking for new ways to understand even the most common things. You have permission.

4 – to love the bully

If you have the opportunity to go to sleep-away camp as an adult, I recommend doing it. You learn a lot about yourself when you are sleeping in a bunk bed and sharing a bathroom for three nights. It was every bit as fun and as traumatic as you imagine. Think of it as a "growth opportunity."

The women in our troop were from all walks of life, all ages, shapes, and sizes. What we had in common was an ongoing dialogue with some aspect of ourselves that convinced us quite frequently that we were somehow not enough. It was different for everyone, but none of us was free of the chatter of the Committee.

During a personal development workshop, I was invited to step way out of my comfort zone to read something aloud from my journal.

As it happened, I had recently written my Committee a letter. I thanked it for its service in keeping me safe.

I offered it love and compassion before telling it that I would no longer need it. I was moving on.

It didn't take long for our facilitator to comment (with disapproval) on just how odd it was that I had thanked the Committee. How strange it was that I had offered it compassion and even love.

The practice among the veteran campers was to shame the voice of the Committee. The idea was to think of the most disagreeable thing imaginable when you heard the voice. It was an aversion tactic.

We learned that one camp veteran had years before begun a practice of addressing the Committee as "Maggot Mouth."

When I heard that, the little voice that lives in my heart (the one that knows things on a level of awareness that exists beyond reason) said, "No!" I didn't have words for it, so I sat down to let my heart and my mind process things.

What I finally realized (weeks after camp) is that the Committee is a bully. A bully who just wants to be loved. It doesn't want to be called Maggot Mouth.

Even the cheesiest Afterschool Special (remember those from the 70's & 80's?) will tell you that the best way to make a bully disappear is to turn her into a friend.

Every bully is just afraid and needs love - especially the bully that lives in your own head. Since you can't escape her, you might as well try befriending her. You don't do that by becoming a bully yourself and calling her Maggot Mouth. That is hating you for hating yourself. At best, it's like throwing matches on a fire to get it to burn out faster (nonsensical). At worst, it's like dousing a fire with gasoline (catastrophic destruction).

When you hear that voice telling you that you are not enough (not smart enough, skinny enough, strong enough, tough enough) - just give it more love. Heap it on. Don't shame the voice. Don't belittle it. Respond with *I love you*. It works like a charm.

Say, for example, the voice in your head starts body shaming you. Ask, "What would I say to my best friend if I heard her speaking like that about herself?"

Would you look at her and call her Maggot Mouth? Or would you tell her that you love her?

Treat yourself the way you would treat your best friend. Respond with understanding and compassion. All you have to do is say, "I love you." You might even say, "You're beautiful."

The first thing that happens is that you distract your brain from the self-hate with the love. We are simple creatures that can only hold one thought at a time.

Next, you develop a habit of triggering love any time you look in the mirror and start body-shaming yourself.

Eventually you may get to the point where you look in the mirror, skip the body shaming, and jump straight to love.

No body issues, you say? It works on any Bully in your head. Try it on the one that tells you that you suck at your job, the one that says you're not a good enough parent, the one that tells you that you shouldn't falter when the shit hits the fan. They all just want love, and they want it from you.

Give the Bully what it wants: your attention and your love. That doesn't make you weak. It makes you strong. It makes you kind. It makes you a bigger, better, more loving and compassionate person. One who can move through the world with a peaceful confidence that becomes contagious.

You have permission to love the Committee. You have permission to love all of you (especially the part that doesn't know how to ask for it). You have permission to act with compassion toward yourself, even if that isn't the conventional wisdom. You have permission to try a new approach.

p.s.

If you happen to be a person who wants to be less judgmental of other people, this is also *your* secret weapon.

Have you ever judged yourself for being judgmental? Again, we are throwing gasoline on a fire. When you hear that voice in your head saying negative things about people (be they people you love or random strangers) - and you are aware enough to know it is happening - don't scold yourself for being so judgey.

(I like to make up words. It's okay to judge me.)

Hear the Bully in your head, and send her some love. Empathize with her. If you have the time, maybe have a conversation to see what is triggering her. Whatever you do, remember that the bully just wants to be loved. Don't be afraid. You're not going to make yourself more judgmental by not scolding yourself. The more that you can accept and love yourself (and your inner judge), the more you can accept and love other people.

You have permission to stop judging yourself for being judgmental.

5 – to hold space for yourself

A *doula* is a woman trained to soothe and support an expectant mother (physically and emotionally) before, during, and after childbirth. She will be there through the pain, the tears, the difficult decisions - simply supporting without judgment. She has no control, no agenda beyond the health of mother & baby.

A doula was the first person I ever heard say, "I will hold space for you."

It's kind of a touchy-feely thing to say, and as a result it can be hard to define. This is my favorite explanation of holding space:

> It means that we are willing to walk alongside another person in whatever journey they're on without judging them, making them feel inadequate, trying to fix them, or trying to impact the outcome. When we hold space for other people, we open our hearts, offer unconditional support, and let go of judgment and control.[*]

---

[*] Plett, Heather. "What It Means to "Hold Space" for People, plus Eight Tips on How to Do It Well." *Heather Plett*. N.p., 22 Aug. 2016. Web. 06 Feb. 2017.

Given that description, it seems fitting that a doula was the one who introduced me to the concept. A doula assumes no control, and has no investment in the *way* that the mother gets through her delivery.

She creates and maintains a safe space in the *most* vulnerable hours of life.

-

I believe strongly in building a community of people in our lives who will celebrate us when we are on top, and provide a safe space for us to land when we fall. Picture it as a series of circus nets set up below you. Some are taut and you can bounce off of them to move your way up - like trampolines. Other nets are there to provide the give you need for a safe landing should you fall. Together they form your *network* (see what I did there?).

One thing is certain. Life is full of ups *and* downs. Eventually, we all take a fall. Ideally, you have access to the right kind of net when you do. In my experience, it doesn't always happen that way. It's kind of like expecting the idyllic childhood that I described at the very beginning of this book. Maybe you exist in a place where you are always supported in just the right way, at just the right time. You're never kicked when you are down. You always get the perfect advice to optimize your recovery from a fall. Let me give you my number. I'd like to join your network.

Here on Earth there are times when the right net is not available. They may be having a crisis of their own. They may not be able to relate to the issue that you're having. They may be on vacation. *You* maybe be on vacation. The problem may be *with your net* (because friends and family sometimes get sick, fight, or fall away). Whatever the reason, and <u>without blame</u>, there are times when you are completely vulnerable and your network is not available.

What do we do when we are at our most vulnerable and we feel that there is no safe place to land? We may try denying that we are vulnerable. We may tell ourselves that we are fine, that the situation isn't really all that bad, and that other people have it much worse. Our Committee may tell us that we *should not* feel this way. We may begin to feel *shame* on top of our vulnerability. All of this makes it very difficult to heal from whatever has caused our pain, our fall, in the first place.

In times like these, it would be lovely to have a life doula. Someone to stay out of our way when we are doing well, and then - when shit gets real, and we are totally raw and exposed - have that person step in. Not to judge us or how we got there, not to give advice. Someone to simply create and maintain a safe space in the most vulnerable hours of life so that we feel safe enough to do the emotional work that we need to do in order to get back on our feet.

We can start by aspiring to be that person, that life doula, in the lives that we touch. Learning to hold space for others is a wonderful thing. I believe it is the kindest thing that we can do for another human being.

What can you do for yourself? It's like my dear friend says, "Holding space for yourself is next level work."

Why next level? It's a multi-stage process.

1. You have to be aware that there is a Committee.
2. You have to be able to PQRS them.

3. You must strip the situation that you're in of any *meaning* or *shame* that comes up due to CRAMPS.
4. You have to *love the bully* that is telling you that you *should* be doing things differently.
5. Release control over the situation.
6. Then, you have to offer yourself unconditional, nonjudgmental compassion & loving-kindness.
7. Lather, rinse and repeat (as the old shampoo bottles would say). Do it over and over and over again.

That's a lot of work. It is especially difficult when you are in the middle of a crisis and probably not functioning at your peak.

We have all been down. We have all known loss. We have all felt very vulnerable and fragile.

Whether it is a literal death, the end of a relationship, a missed opportunity, or the closing of a chapter in your life, we are all too familiar with the hollow feeling that accompanies loss.

*We all deal with loss differently. There is no right way to grieve. I am not qualified to tell you how to do it, and I wouldn't be holding space for you if I did.

I can offer you an observation and a tool.

I have observed that we tell ourselves that we should "get over it." We think that we should have control over the magnitude and/or the timeline of our grief. Instead of holding space for ourselves to have good days and bad days (which we will have regardless), we turn bad days even worse by bullying ourselves into believing that we're grieving wrong, or that we shouldn't be grieving at all.

Here's the tool: presence.

Check out that list above. Take yourself through all of the steps. Be aware of when you are fragile, when you are suffering. Be aware of when you are grieving. Watch the Committee find it's way into your internal dialogue. Is it telling you that you are alone, and/or that the magnitude or duration (or simple existence) of your grief is inappropriate? PQRS that noise! Love

---

*If you are in crisis, or feeling suicidal, contact your doctor, therapist, a crisis hotline or a hospital immediately.

yourself like you would love your dearest friend, your closest family.

We have to feel our feelings before we can move beyond them. We can't bottle them up in the name of *should* or *should not*. We can't choose how and when we feel loss.

Instead, we can choose *how* we will deal with our feelings. I'm not inviting you to wallow needlessly or pity yourself. I *am* saying - feelings happen. Hold space for yourself to have them.

When the situation requires, allow yourself to be the net that provides the give to soften the fall. Create a safe space for yourself to be in when you are your most vulnerable. Don't try to solve the feelings. Situations can be changed, work can be done, conditions can be improved, care can be taken - but *feelings cannot be solved*. Allow yourself the time to feel what you are feeling without judging it.

You have permission to hold space for yourself.

Holding space for yourself means that you are willing to walk alongside yourself on whatever journey you're on without judging, feeling inadequate, or trying to "fix" yourself. When you hold space for yourself, you open your heart, offer unconditional support, and let go of judgment and the illusion of control over your feelings.

6 – to be an adventurer

You have permission to be an adventurer!

What does this mean?

1. No matter where you are on the path, you are never lost.
2. Every step forward is a step in the right direction.
3. There is no finish line.

Here's the thing. You only feel lost when you aren't where you think you're *supposed to be*.

Remove that condition and, no matter where you find yourself, you're simply an adventurer in uncharted territory. You're a person taking life as it comes, making the best of the situation you're in.

By all means - set goals, dream, be a responsible human being. Live your life in a way that affords you the opportunity to be generous in every way possible.

Also realize that along the way, <u>you are going to be detoured</u>. Your plans are going to change.

The destination you had in mind may no longer seem as desirable, and you may change your itinerary. Life may throw you and your travel party the equivalent of dysentery on the Oregon Trail (cheesy computer game from the 80's).

Here's another analogy: you have a choice about how you see things when the train derails. You can panic because the train was taking you from A to B in a nice straight line and now there is NO WAY you are going to get to the station on schedule. Or you can be grateful that you survived the derailment, grab your backpack, dust off the rubble, and take in the sights where you are. Decide what the next right thing is, make a friend, and enjoy some of the local fare while you're there. What can you learn from the experience? It's a growth opportunity.

When you allow yourself to be on an adventure, detours are just opportunities to have unanticipated experiences.

You say to yourself, "Plot twist!" Then, you keep moving forward.

I also like to say, "There is no finish line."

What do I mean? Well, does any of this sound familiar?

- when I get my diploma
- when I get my dream job
- when I get a raise
- when I find the right partner
- when the kids grow up
- when I have my loans paid off
- when I retire
- when I...

If we're always looking for the finish line, we're always going to be disappointed because it just keeps moving.

If our focus is always ahead of us searching for Joy on the other side of the finish line, we do not realize that Joy is running right beside us. We just need to be present to see it.

For me, the daily endeavor is to keep setting new goals and enjoy the *adventure* of working toward achieving them (whether or not I actually do: see detour & derailment analogies above).

We get to keep learning, keep growing, keep on loving each other, and ourselves in new fresh ways each and every day.

There are milestones, achievements, accomplishments, and countless reasons to celebrate ourselves in all that we do. There is no finish line.

Adventuring places us in the present moment and reminds us to enjoy it, rather than allowing ourselves to feel lost. Rather than always looking ahead to how marvelous life will be *when I...*

You have permission to be an adventurer!

7 – to acknowledge that you are a creator

Have you seen the classic Jimmy Stewart movie *It's a Wonderful Life*?

In case you haven't or you need a refresher, it's the story of George Bailey. George is a man who dreams of travel and adventure, but through various twists of fate spends his entire life in his small, sleepy hometown of Bedford Falls. He runs his family's Building & Loan. He keeps the community growing and the doors open even through the Great Depression. He protects the interests of the town from the greedy skinflint Mr. Potter who would see the Building & Loan shut down. Without George keeping Potter in check, the results (which we get a glimpse of through movie magic) would be Pottersville: a slum where the only person who thrives is Potter.

When calamity strikes and $8000 disappears, George considers taking his own life (worth more dead than alive with his life insurance policy). An angel named Clarence ultimately saves him. Clarence gives him a view of what the world would be like if George had never been born. In a world without George, some people have died, others have gone to prison, and Pottersville is a reality. His friends' lives are in ruin. His children, of course, do not exist without him.

He glimpses that although he thought his life was a mundane waste and ultimately a failure, he was actually responsible for creating opportunities and bringing joy to more lives than he had ever imagined possible.

I have seen that movie more than a dozen times. I got the message (or thought I did): You touch more lives than you realize, and it's a wonderful life. Yada yada, pass the eggnog.

I have subtly reframed the moral of this classic story. It has made all of the difference.

George Bailey thought he was a banker.

Really, he was a creator and a light worker who worked at a bank.

At various times in my life, I have thought I was a student, a receptionist, an activities director, a resident advisor, an executive assistant, a teacher's aide, a library assistant, a personal trainer, a life coach, a small business owner, a writer, and a poet.

I realized something very recently. I am a creator and a light worker who merely worked at all of those things.

The same is true of you.

No matter how you keep busy (working, learning, parenting, surviving), no matter what label you wear (professional, student, parent, awesome human) - you are creating. Most adults will claim that they are not creative; but they create their lives, their careers, their families, their homes, their landscapes, their menus, and their wardrobe. They CREATE! Who is to say what is worthy of calling "creative" and what is not? Every action taken (or inaction) is an act that creates the life you live.

You are creating a reality for yourself, and the people you know. Even destruction is a form of creation. And if you believe that your circumstances are so far outside of anything creative, understand this: you have the opportunity to create your perspective, your next step, your reactions to the world around you.

You get to create the energy that you bring into each moment, each room you enter, each conversation that you have.

If you are doing it with a smile on your face and/or a song in your heart, you're a light-worker, too. You bring light to a stranger with a smile or a kind word. You bring light to a friend with a phone call or a warm embrace. You bring light to your family with the love that you give and the time that you share. Each time that you do one of these things, you're bringing light into the world, making it a better place, and filling it with good vibrations.

Once you start to see that you have the power to create, the power to bring light into the world by being your naturally loving self, you start to realize the power you have.

You are a creator. You are a light-worker. This is who you are.

The *job* that you have is simply *what you do*.

You are a creator and a light-worker who is busy doing the job of:

Doctor, actor, artist, lawyer, mother, flight attendant, janitor, sailor, teacher, pilot, engineer, musician, surfer, father, nonprofit director, soldier, computer scientist, telemarketer, office manager, CFO, reindeer farmer, underwater basket weaver...

There are as many ways to be a creator and a light-worker as there are amazing humans on planet Earth. You are doing it right.

You have permission to acknowledge that you are a creator.

You bring light to the world just by being in it.

Thank you.

8 – to create your own echo chamber

Allow me to introduce you to your echo chamber.

The waves of an explosion will become magnified and concussive in an enclosed space – ripples bouncing and ricocheting off of each other. This is true in our homes and our minds, too.

The words that we use matter.

Having them bouncing around in our heads and our homes magnifies their effects.

With that in mind, let's choose our words with care.

You're learning to love the bully. You're quieting the voices of the Committee.

If we can all do that, our ripples will change the face of the world.

It's part of being a creator and a light-worker.

Let's create some joyful noise for those echo chambers of ours.

I discovered my echo chamber quite by accident. I started repeating a few sentences to my kids. I wanted them to hear these refrains of positivity.
- You are an amazing human being.
- I appreciate you.
- I adore you.
- I'm listening.
- I'm sorry.

I would say those things often to create an echo of love, gratitude and sincerity in our home and in their heads. Eventually, they started saying those things to each other and back to me. And then, the magic happened. I started speaking those words to myself:
- You are an amazing human being.
- I appreciate you.
- I adore you.
- I'm listening.
- I'm sorry.

It was transformational.

So this is a permission slip and an invitation to you. If you don't like what you hear echoed in your home and in your head, you have permission to create your own echo. I invite you to borrow these sentences, or make up your own.

In my experience, I had to say them to someone else (my family) before I was able to hear them in my own head. You can start wherever you need to. Start with pets, friends, family, or in your own beautiful mind. Start with sticky notes on your mirror or your computer. Use bath crayons on your shower wall. There's no wrong way to create beautiful ripples in the world.

Give it a try. You have permission to create your own echo chamber.

9 – to ask yourself powerful questions

Have you ever had someone ask you a simple question that totally reframed your thinking? This is how it happened for me...

I was wrapping up a certification (another milestone on my adventure as a creator). I was discussing my next steps with a friend who was embarking on a career as a life coach. I told her that though I was looking forward to sharing my new expertise, my kids were still young and plans to use my certification to do "something fabulous" would wait until they were a bit older.

She asked me this question: "What does fabulous look like?"

That question stopped me in my tracks. What *did* fabulous look like? It looked like whatever the heck I wanted it to look like, didn't it? I was the one defining it. It gave me freedom - it gave me *permission* - to create a model that fit my lifestyle while being *fabulously* fulfilling.

In coach-speak what she asked me was a "powerful question." The results can be transformative when someone you trust asks you to get outside of your head for a minute and shift your perspective.

The fact is, even if you are fortunate enough to have a life coach, they can't be with you 24/7. Sometimes you just need a little reframing. I've found the best way to do that is to ask myself a few powerful questions.

Powerful questions can help you: get unstuck, set goals, commit, refocus, celebrate, and cultivate self-discovery.

Note: One of my favorite things about life coaches is that is their job to assume that the people that they work with are creative, resourceful, and whole.

As you ask yourself these questions, assume that you are CREATIVE, RESOURCEFUL AND WHOLE! Why? Because you ARE!! You have the answers. You just have to ask the right questions.

Of course this permission slip goes hand in hand with *permission to be curious*. This is about being curious about *yourself*. The same rules apply. There are no stupid questions. In fact, some of the best questions are the ones that seem kind of obvious or silly.

- What does achieving your goal look (or feel) like?
- What's the next step?
- What about this is important to you?
- What else?
- What have you learned? How can that help you moving forward?

Here are a few of my other favorites:

- Where did that belief come from, is it real? (Challenge the CRAMPS.)
- How would life be different if you truly believed in yourself?
- What choices do you need to make to achieve your goal?
- Why is it important? And then, why is *that* important. And then, why...

And of course...
- What does fabulous look like?

Do you feel like you don't know the answers? This one is awesome:

- If you did know the answer, what would it be?

It is amazing how that question unlocks your brain, and gives you permission to say that thing that you were feeling tentative about because you thought it might be wrong.

Type *powerful coaching questions* into your favorite search engine and you will find literally hundreds of these life-changing questions.

You have permission to take the time to ask yourself powerful questions, and trust that YOU HAVE THE ANSWERS. You are creative, resourceful and whole. You've got this!

One more thing: Writing your answer on paper gives you the opportunity to really think it through, as well as giving you the opportunity to look back and reflect. Let your answer provoke the next powerful question.

10 – to get out of your own way

This is the beginning and the end of giving yourself permission. Every single permission slip is working you closer to the goal of getting out of your own way.

I was on a road trip with a couple of amazing girlfriends. We were driving through the middle of the desert - headed home from a wonderful day in Sedona. We were talking about personal crossroads and opportunities ahead. We were laughing about how sometimes it seems like a door opens, and still we hesitate to walk through it.

I conjured this image of myself for my companions:

> So there I am. Opportunity has left the door wide open for me to walk through.
> I say, "Hang on just a minute, Opportunity.
> Let me get my purse.
> Oh, and my sunglasses.
> And I'm going to need my phone.
> And maybe a jacket. You never know.
> Do I need a hat?

It might be a good idea to bring some snacks.
And a water bottle.
And of course I will need some comfortable shoes."

I grab my tennis shoes and tie them.
To. Each. Other.

We all had a good laugh at ourselves as I detailed how I quite literally trip myself up when all I really have to do is walk through the door with a little faith that Opportunity has it covered from there. That's why the door was open in the first place.

Does this sound vaguely familiar? It isn't exactly self-sabotage. It's simply an inability to let go of the illusion of control and trust that the perfect outcome is available.

What I really needed was to give myself permission to just walk through that door: to have a little faith and get out of my own way.

You have permission to get out of your own way.

You have permission to laugh at yourself when you can't seem to do it, too. Sometimes that laughter - that awareness - is just the kick in the pants you need to push you through the door and on to what Opportunity has waiting for you on the other side.

11 – to go alone

Very early on our communities tell us that there is safety in numbers. Human babies are helpless and require constant care. As the label on every piece of baby gear manufactured in the last 25 years advises: DO NOT LEAVE CHILD UNATTENDED AT ANY TIME.

We know that we should find a buddy, stay with the group, and never wander off alone. As we get older we may find a best friend, a boyfriend or girlfriend. We pair off. It is socially acceptable to have a companion for dances, dinners, concerts and movies.

It is the black sheep of the herd that shows up unaccompanied. Other. *The Loner.* Maybe your Committee tells you that being alone *means* something – even if you're not sure exactly what. Whatever it is, it's not good.

Whether it is because of death, divorce, or a simple desire to spend some time discovering who you are when you are not committed to spending all of your time with another human – you may find yourself alone.

As time goes by, I meet more and more people who find themselves flying solo (so to speak). These are all strong independent people who participate and thrive in their communities.

They are not lonely. They have lives and friends. Their friends have lives, too. They're not always available to come out and play.

As a result, there are occasions when there is something to do, but no one to do it with. Sometimes that means that they will pass on an event that they might have really enjoyed.

It seems especially difficult to go to a movie or say "table for one" when you find yourself on the other side of a long-term relationship. Aside from being socially awkward, you're used to having your best buddy beside you.

A friend of mine recently told me (nearly 6 years after her divorce): "There is a concert coming up that I want to go to, and none of my friends are available that weekend, so I bought one ticket. I gave myself permission to go alone and enjoy myself."

Just the act of buying that single ticket was empowering. She realized that though it felt weird, it wasn't lonely. It felt good to decide that there was something that she wanted to do and to do it happily (with or without a companion). It was a simple personal declaration of independence.

I know that this won't resonate with everyone. For some it may seem obvious, and for others it may seem unnecessary.

But, if your lack of a buddy has kept you from doing something that you can safely do alone – this is for you. With love.

You are an adventurer. Enjoy what the world has to offer you (with or without a companion).

Don't let opportunities to experience Joy fall away because your Committee has you afraid that there is something wrong with a table for one.

You have permission to go alone.

12 – to create Door Number Three

Black or White. Right or Wrong. Stay or Go.

Our minds - our Committees - are very comfortable with this type of thinking. It is very straightforward. It carries with it the illusion of efficiency.

Is it any wonder that our brains are wired to think this way? Surviving as a species, it was a good thing for our primitive brain to have only two things to choose from. It's that animal part of ourselves – our lizard brain (not a lot of higher-level thinking going on inside of a lizard's head). Survival is the name of the game. Fight or Flight. You don't want to stand around considering alternatives for too long when you are prey.

It shouldn't be surprising that when we are physically and emotionally taxed (feeling pretty lizardy) we are not in our most creative space. We are not prey, but our lizard brain doesn't realize it. Yet now that we are out of the cave, these are often the times when we can benefit the most from at least one more (not always obvious) option. A Door Number Three.

What is Door Number Three?
Let's look at it in terms of Black or White. Door Number Three can be:
- Splitting things up: Black today, White tomorrow. Everybody gets a turn.
- A melding of the options: Grey.
- Something totally different: Red, Purple, Green or Blue.
- Deciding that you don't want to color at all.

Remember you are a creator.

Any time that you think that you have no good option, there is a very good chance that your lizard brain is thinking for you.

This is when it can be handy to PQRS:

- Be Present
- Quiet the Committee
- Release/Reframe
- Start over

If you can be present enough to realize that you believe that there are only two options, you can quiet and calm your inner reptile long enough to release that belief and reframe your situation. Start over with the knowledge that you have permission to create a Door Number Three.

Door Number Three is also useful for escaping the bonds of perfectionism. If you've put off doing something because you're sure that it has to be done perfectly or not done at all, try creating Door Number Three. Do the best that you can and embrace the delightful imperfection that comes with being human.

Remember: It isn't going to be perfect. You have permission to bumble and stumble.

If you anticipate a conflict and believe that things can only go one of two ways – try to imagine a third possibility. You even don't have to know what it is. Just be open to it.

All you have to do is create space for that Door Number Three. You don't have to know what's behind it right away. Simply be aware that there is (almost) always another possibility.

There are times in our lives when we really are placed between a rock and a hard place. When that happens, we still get to choose how we will respond. We still get to choose the energy that we bring to that difficult situation.

When you get stumped, and can't think of another way to create Door Number Three, choose a Permission Slip that fits:
- allow yourself grace
- make noise and take up space
- be curious
- love the bully
- be an adventurer
- acknowledge that you are a creator
- create your own echo chamber
- ask yourself powerful questions
- get out of your own way
- go alone

You have permission to create Door Number Three.

13 – to be your own Permission Slip Ninja

What you hold in your hand – these are the permission slips that I have written my children, my friends, and myself. There are so many more to be written.

Remember, you are a creator.

Open your heart and your mind. Change the way you think.

Ask yourself, "What do I want permission to do?"

Some of the things that come to mind may be variations of those that I've shared. Some will be entirely your own. Only you know what you need to give yourself permission to do.

Here are a few things for you to keep in mind as you create them:
- Act from your highest, most compassionate self.
- Maintain your obligations, pay your bills on time, and care for your people.
- Be aware of the effect your actions will have, and do no harm (to yourself or others).

Only use your powers for the good of yourself and others, my friends.

Here are a few ideas to play with. Permission:
- to embrace abundance so that you can share it.
- to find work that makes your heart sing.
- to love your deepest imperfections.
- to find beauty in every situation.
- to try grow and learn and fail and grow again.
- to play.
- to say no.
- to call yourself photographer, writer, poet, artist (even if you're not getting paid).

You have permission to explore your heart and your mind. Discover the ways that your Committee has been holding you back (with love and concern for your well-being). Thank it for its service. Be Present. Quiet the Committee. Release the old ideas that have held you back. Start over with new permissions to thrive in an infinite number of ways.

V – When the Struggle is REAL

We have a strategy for dealing with the hypothetical Committee, right? PQRS the heck out of them, write any number of permission slips to outwit their nay saying, and THRIVE!

But what about when the Committee is real?

Follow me on a journey.

The road meanders a bit, but we're headed someplace good.

I recall that when I was first introduced to the idea of personifying my negative self-talk, it was compared to an undesirable roommate in my head.

"Would you let your roommate speak to you that way?"

Of course not.

The recommendation was to treat that roommate's voice as you would treat thoughts during meditation. Simply notice the sound and return to breath.

This may come as a shock to you, but that didn't work. My roommate would not be evicted by my breath. (Insert halitosis joke here.)

Later, someone suggested that I give the voice a name and persona. That gave me the ability to directly tell that character that it shouldn't speak to me that way. "Hush your mouth, Mrs. Meanie Face. You're not the boss of me."

Again – I had no success. Now I just had some weird, mean lady living in my head.

At last, I realized that the voice was not a single cry, but a chorus. That helped. The chorus sang out in unison with a single message, but the voices were many.

The thoughts weren't originally mine. They'd merely been dropped in my ear; like a song that I just couldn't get out of my head.

Surely, that has happened to you. The song is in your head and no one else can hear it. But, you didn't write it, perform it, produce or distribute it. You certainly aren't collecting royalty checks.

You're just an innocent victim of a catchy hook from someone else's favorite guilty pleasure band. Except in the case of the Committee, there's no snappy beat. It's just a nasty voicemail on repeat that is pummeling your soul.

Once I realized that it was a band of voices, I decided that I wanted to know exactly who the "front men" were. Now and then someone had a solo; and I could recognize his or her distinct voice. Yes – there are always going to be no name back-up singers that are just part of the chorus. But some of these people I actually knew.

They were real. They were alive. They were in my life.

What do you do when you realize that your Committee has people you love sitting at the head of the table?

I don't know if there is a right thing. I did what I do. I began to write.

I wrote them a letter that they'd never receive. Because as my Sister Friend likes to say, "You don't have to announce the revolution."

Dear Committee,

You have formed and informed so much of my personality.

Who would I be if I had not been taught to doubt so many aspects of myself at such a tender age?

What might I have been if I had not surrendered my sense of worth to you in so many ways?

Maybe better. Maybe worse. I can't know. In any case, I am grateful. I love who I am today.

And. And now, it is time to say goodbye.

While I have grown and worked to embrace my magnificently whole and imperfect self, you have remained firmly set in your narrow beliefs.

You point to the futility of dreaming. You make note of other people's failures as though they are cautionary tales.

I am ready to dream!

I am ready to try and fail and learn and grow and dream again and again and again.

There is no place for you in my dreams.

I won't play small for your dark audience. That time has ended. Now, I shine my light on you.

You represent the villagers who shame those who would travel beyond the pale. You celebrate the failure of those who return broken as victories in your own small mind.

I'm off to explore - unencumbered by the weight of your fears.

The lightness I feel is immense and disorienting.

Had I known this was possible, I'd have cut you loose decades ago.

But then I would not be who I am today; and today I love myself.

So thank you, Committee. I bid you farewell knowing that whatever happens next, I will thrive.

With love, compassion & gratitude.

That letter is my personal PQRS to the Committee voices that belong to people I know. It changed my life and started a journey that I am thrilled to be on.

So – with love and compassion and gratitude – do what you do. Write a letter, a poem, or a song. Paint a picture, take a hike and throw a rock in a lake, light some flash paper and watch it disappear before your eyes. Find a way to symbolically release those bitches to nature with a smile on your face and a song in your heart.

And.

Do it with the knowledge that Sister Friend knows what she's talking about. You don't have to announce the revolution. It's usually better if you don't. This is for your gain, not for you to cause anyone else pain. You don't need to become a member of anyone else's Committee bringing him or her down.

-

Now – what happens when a voice from the head of the Committee comes into your real life, pulls up a real chair at the dinner table, and starts in with their real mouth?

That, as they say, is a horse of a different color.

Real life Committee members can be like X-ray radiation. A little exposure gets a job done and can serve an important purpose. Too much can burn you and leave you for dead.

It's your Committee and you have to decide what exposure dosage is safe. Figure out what your metaphorical lead apron looks like and protect your gonads.

Use the Door Number Three permission slip. You are a creator, a light-worker. Come up with a new strategy for dealing with real life Committee members.

Allow yourself grace. Remember that you have a voice and take up an appropriate amount of space. Stay curious. Hold space for yourself. Create the positive energy that you carry in to the room. Bring your light. Write whatever permission slip you need to come away whole.

Realize that *they* are under the influence of their own Committee Responsible for Assigning Meaning and Provoking Shame. If you think that their voice is loud in your head, know that it is deafening in *theirs*.

The other thing to keep in mind is – you know what the Committee is, how it got there, and how to quiet it. They don't. So, when you can, begin and end your encounter with quiet compassion for yourself and them.

Also understand that, whether directed at yourself or anyone else, compassion and pity come across very differently.

Compassion feels like *holding space*. It is gentle, nonjudgmental, and openhearted.

Pity feels like putting up a wall. It is feeling sorry for the condition of another as compared to you (or vice versa). Someone is better, and someone is worse.

None of us wants to be pitied, but we could all use a whole lot more compassion.

VI – The Beginning

You are a creator and a light-worker first and always. No matter what you are doing.

You have a shiny new toolbox that is loaded with tools. Loaded, but not full. Never full - always room for more.

What Permission Slips will you write for yourself?

What Permission Slips will you write for the people that you love?

There are only adventures ahead.
No finish line in sight.
Remember – that's a good thing.

You are never lost.
You are creative, resourceful and whole.

What you will do? Where will this journey lead you?

You are invited to begin as this book ends.

And this book will end as it began:

> If we could change ourselves, the tendencies in the world would also change. As a man changes his own nature, so does the attitude of the world change toward him. We need not wait to see what others do.
> — Mahatma Gandhi

The waiting is over.

This is your call to action.

This is your adventure.

> And above all, watch with glittering eyes the whole world around you because the greatest secrets are always hidden in the most unlikely places. Those who don't believe in magic will never find it.
> — Roald Dahl

Believe in *your* magic.

This is your permission.

This is the beginning.

The next page is yours to fill.

It is pure possibility.

So are you.

This Page Is Intentionally Left Blank

(I've always loved the ridiculous irony of that.)

Made in the USA
San Bernardino, CA
05 June 2017